MAXIMIZING YOUR PROFITS
& UNLOCK TAX CREDITS

MELANIE E. LEWIS

Copyright ©2025 by Melanie E. Lewis
Maximizing Your Profits & Unlock Tax Credits

Paperback ISBN: 979-8-9994619-3-3

Publisher:
CoolBird Publishing House
publish@coolbirdstudios.com
www.coolbirdstudios.com

All rights reserved. No part of this publication may be reproduced, stored in a retrieval system, or transmitted in any form or by any means – electronic, mechanical, digital, photocopy, recording, or any other -except for brief quotations in printed reviews, without the prior permission of the author. Please purchase only authorized copies. References for resources used have been placed in the back of this book. Bulk copies can be purchased thru the author.

Printed in the United States of America.

Dedication

To every visionary & entrepreneur who's ever been underestimated...May you build boldly and profit wisely.

Acknowledgments

This journey has not been mine alone...First and foremost, I thank my incredible children Breanna, Nathanael, and Hannah who inspire me daily with their strength, laughter, and love. You are my greatest blessings, and everything I build is with you in mind.

To my favorite uncle, Marlon, thank you for always seeing the best in me and reminding me of who I am, even when I forget. Your wisdom and belief have been a steady foundation.

To my dear brother, the one who set the bar high, thank you for showing me what excellence looks like. You've always led with quiet strength, and I'm grateful for your example.

To my beloved mother, Brenda Lewis who was a principal accountant for the City of Detroit, we spoke the same financial language. You raised me with the tools, mindset, and principles that would one day shape the foundation of everything I do. Your influence laid the groundwork for the calling I now walk in. Though you're no longer here, your wisdom and example are present in every client I serve and every business I help build.
I carry your legacy with honor and deep purpose.

To Treva and Doris, thank you for your unwavering encouragement. Your support has pushed me through tough seasons and reminded me of the mission I'm here to fulfill.

This book would not have been possible without the support of my family, my team at Empowered Dominion Network, and the countless entrepreneurs and visionaries I've had the privilege to coach over the years.

Thank you to those who shared their testimonials, insights, and encouragement. To my readers thank you for taking this journey with me. Your success is my purpose. Let's continue building empowered, profitable, and purpose driven businesses together.

And to everyone who has poured into me; my friends, clients, mentors, and silent cheerleaders thank you. Your faith, feedback, and fuel have carried me further than words can capture. This book is a result of every lesson, every late night, and every leap of faith.
Thank you for walking this journey with me.

BEFORE WE BEGIN

Being an entrepreneur is not easy. It takes courage, resilience, and a willingness to learn. By focusing on maximizing your profits and unlocking tax credits, you're stacking the deck in your favor. You're ensuring that your hard work translates into financial reward and stability. That means more peace of mind, more ability to invest in your dreams, and more impact you can make through your business.

As a nationally respected business strategist and tax expert, I've seen firsthand the transformation that occurs when entrepreneurs take control of their financial destiny. It's my hope that the knowledge and strategies in this book empower you to do just that. Equip yourself, take action, and watch your business prosper. Here's to your success and to every dollar of profit you earn and keep!

TESTIMONIALS

"Starting Evansville Pathway Home was challenging, but Ms. Lewis's guidance made it much easier. Her expertise in tax laws and regulations was incredibly helpful. Ms. Lewis provided excellent advice on tax planning and structuring, which helped build a strong foundation for my business. She understood my vision and made sure every financial decision supported my long-term goals. She made complex tax concepts easy to understand with clear explanations, boosting my confidence and helping me make informed decisions. Her proactive approach to tax compliance prevented issues, ensuring Evansville Pathway Home stayed on track with tax authorities. Her attention to detail and thoroughness were crucial for our success.

Ms. Lewis's support went beyond professional expertise; she genuinely cared about my business's success, fostering a trusting partnership. I highly recommend Ms. Lewis to any entrepreneur looking for a great tax strategist. Her guidance was vital in realizing my dream, and I am deeply grateful for her help. Evansville Pathway Home owes much of its success to Ms. Lewis, and I believe her expertise will benefit many future business owners."

-Alonte Thomas, Owner
Evansville Pathway Home

"I started working with Melanie over 4 years ago once I decided to become an entrepreneur. Melanie is very strong minded and knowledgeable about the business world. Working with Mel has been nothing short of successful. Since becoming a student of Melanie, I've learned how to structure my business properly and I've also learned how to receive business funding for my starter businesses. Working alongside Mel on a consistent basis while allowing her to guide me has sent my business from rock bottom to top tier. I can't wait to see what my new business journey looks like."

Sharita Woods, Founder
Ree-Liable Property Management LLC

"Melanie Lewis resolved my 2023 state tax dilemma. Her expertise resulted in a net gain of over $6,500. She tackled complex tax liabilities other larger companies couldn't."

Eddie – New Paradigm
Repeat Customer

Contents

PART I: FOUNDATION & STRATEGY

Chapter 1   **Understanding Your Business Structure:** Discover the tax and legal advantages of choosing the right entity for your goals.. 9

Chapter 2   **Organizing Your Financials for Success:** Learn how proper bookkeeping, banking, and reporting impact your profits.. 15

Chapter 3   **The Profit Formula: Revenue, Write-Offs, and ROI:** Explore strategies to increase income while decreasing unnecessary expenses.. 22

Chapter 4   **Positioning Your Business for Tax Credit Eligibility:** Find out how to access powerful federal and state tax credits designed for growth.. 31

Chapter 5:   **Unlocking the Power of Tax Credits:** A deep dive into employment credits, energy credits, and industry-specific incentives.. 40

PART II: GROWTH, BENEFITS & LEGACY

Chapter 6:   **How to Use Your Business to Benefit YOU:** Turn everyday personal expenses into legal business deductions to enhance your lifestyle.. 47

Chapter 7:   **Creating a Legacy So Your Business Doesn't Stop With You:** Plan for succession, inheritance, and mission continuity beyond your lifetime.. 54

Chapter 8:   **Offering Services That YOU Need- Health, Vision, Dental, & Retirement:** Structure your business to provide health coverage, savings plans, and security for you and your family.. 56

Chapter 9:   **Position Your Business for Global Reach:** Expand your offerings, build an international client base, and multiply your revenue streams.. 61

Chapter 10: **Create a Strong, Self-Sustaining Network:** Develop a community around your brand that generates referrals, support, and long-term growth.. 67

Bonus Checklists & Resources.. 73

Additional Resources: 81

Disclaimer

This book is intended for informational and educational purposes only. The author is a qualified tax professional and has written this material to help readers better understand general tax concepts, common scenarios, and potential strategies. However, this book is not a substitute for personalized advice from a licensed tax advisor, accountant, or attorney.

Some content in this book includes publicly available resources and examples from the Internal Revenue Service (IRS), adapted for educational use. In addition, the author draws upon personal professional experiences, including fictionalized companies and composite scenarios based on real client interactions. All client-related examples have been modified to protect privacy, and any company or individual names are fictional unless otherwise stated.

Because tax laws and regulations frequently change and may vary based on specific circumstances, readers are strongly encouraged to consult a qualified tax professional for tailored guidance.

The author and publisher disclaim any liability, loss, or risk incurred as a consequence, directly or indirectly, of the use and application of any information contained in this book.

Chapter 1

The Profit Mindset – Laying the Foundation

Every entrepreneur starts with a dream perhaps to innovate, to be their own boss, or to change the world. However, turning that dream into a profitable reality requires more than passion; it requires a profit mindset. In this chapter, we'll establish the foundation for maximizing profits in your business which ultimately sets the stage for the tax credit strategies to come.

Profit Over Revenue
It's easy to get caught up in top-line revenue and sales growth, but high revenues mean little if your expenses eat it all. Profit is what truly measures success because it's the money that stays in your business (and your pocket) after all bills and taxes have been paid. Embracing a profit-first mindset means planning for profit intentionally, rather than hoping something is left over. For example, a small retail entrepreneur who was thrilled to hit a $1 million sales milestone, but she was shocked to find her net profit was almost zero. The issue was clear: she treated profit as an afterthought. Together, we reworked her pricing and trimmed unnecessary costs. We also allocated a fixed percentage of every sale to profit (a principle similar to the "Profit First" method). Within a year, her business turned around and she was consistently netting a healthy profit each quarter. The lesson? Focus on profit from the start, not as an afterthought.

The Power of Tax Credits for Your Bottom Line:
What many business owners overlook is that taxes are one of the biggest expenses. This is where tax credits become game-changers. A tax credit is essentially free money from the government that you can use to reduce your tax bill dollar-for-dollar. Imagine you owe $10,000 in taxes, but you qualify for a $3,000 tax credit your tax bill drops to $7,000. That $3,000 goes back into your business's pocket, effectively boosting your profit by $3,000. In other words, every dollar in tax credits is a dollar added to your bottom line. Throughout this book, we will explore how savvy entrepreneurs treat tax strategy as part of their profit strategy.

Mindset Shift -Think Like a Strategist
To maximize profit, start thinking like a strategist. This means regularly asking questions like:

- Where is my money going?
- How can I reduce costs without sacrificing quality?
- How can I earn more from each customer?
- Am I taking advantage of all legal avenues to reduce taxes?

A profit-focused entrepreneur is always on the lookout for inefficiencies to eliminate and opportunities to seize. One founder I advised realized she was spending heavily on express shipping to delight customers with fast delivery. It was a nice perk, but it wiped out her profit margin. By shifting to a reasonable flat-rate shipping (and communicating the change as an eco-friendly choice to reduce waste), customers stayed loyal and her costs plummeted. The saved expenses went straight to profit. Similarly, she discovered a little-known state tax incentive for e-commerce businesses that invest in recycled packaging materials. By switching her packaging (which aligned with her new eco-friendly messaging), she qualified for a tax credit that year that saved her an additional $5,000 in taxes. These moves required a strategic mindset that balanced customer experience with profitability and knowing what incentives are available.

Real-World Example – Turning Losses into Profits:
Consider *Example Manufacturing*, a fictional small manufacturer that was barely breaking even. They had strong sales, but rising costs and hefty tax bills meant the owners took home almost nothing. After adopting a profit mindset, they made two big changes: First, they performed a thorough cost audit and negotiated better rates with suppliers, saving $30,000 a year. Second, they invested in new energy efficient machinery that improved productivity and qualified for an energy efficiency tax incentive, reducing their taxable income and saving them $10,000 in taxes the next year. The combined effect? Their next annual profit jumped from $0 to $40,000. The owners used part of that profit to pay down debt and reinvest in marketing and the business began to thrive. This example shows how reducing costs, increasing efficiency, and leveraging tax credits together create a powerful synergy for your bottom line.

Action Steps – Laying Your Profit Foundation:

- **Know Your Numbers:** Take a hard look at your financial statements. What was your profit last month or last year? Calculate your profit margin (profit divided by revenue) to understand how much of each dollar in sales you actually keep.

- **Set a Profit Goal:** Don't settle for what's left over. Decide on a target profit margin (e.g., 15% or 20%) for your business and treat profit like a non-negotiable expense. This mindset will force you to price appropriately and control costs.

- **Identify Quick Wins:** List one or two expenses you can reduce immediately. (for instance, unused subscriptions or renegotiating a vendor contract). Also, identify one potential tax credit or deduction you might be missing out on, and make a note to explore it in Chapter 2.

- **Commit to Continuous Improvement:** Adopting a profit mindset is not a one-time task. Schedule a monthly or quarterly "profit review" meeting (even if it's just you) to track progress and adjust your strategies. Celebrate the small wins as your profitability improves!

With a solid profit-focused foundation in place, you're ready to dive deeper. In the next chapter, we'll demystify tax credits and incentives which are known as the often overlooked "hidden gold" that can significantly boost your business's profitability.

Key Takeaways

Action Steps I Need to Takeaway

Questions to Ask My Consultant

Ideas for My Business Growth

Chapter 2

Understanding Tax Credits and Incentives

Overview

Taxes can often feel like a burden, but what if you could turn them into a strategic advantage for your business? This chapter uncovers the world of tax credits and incentives. Essentially, money saving opportunities provided by the government to encourage certain business activities. By understanding and utilizing them, you can potentially save thousands of dollars, directly increasing your profit.

Tax Credits vs. Deductions – What's the Difference?

It's important to distinguish between a tax deduction and a tax credit. A deduction reduces your taxable income. For example, if you have a $1,000 deduction and your tax rate is 30%, you save $300 in tax. A credit, on the other hand, reduces your actual tax bill dollar-for-dollar. A $1,000 tax credit saves you $1,000 in tax, regardless of your tax rate. In essence, deductions help you by shrinking the amount of income you pay tax on, while credits help you by directly cutting the tax you owe. Credits are incredibly powerful; some are even refundable (meaning if the credit is bigger than your tax bill, you could get a refund check for the difference), though most business credits are non-refundable (they can reduce your tax to zero, but not below).

Why Do Governments Offer Credits?

Governments use tax credits and incentives to encourage behaviors that are good for the economy or society. For businesses, this can mean incentives for hiring certain groups of people, investing in research, going green, or setting up in certain locations. As an entrepreneur, understanding these incentives is like knowing the rules of a game because you can "score points" (save money) by doing things that also align with your business growth.

Common Tax Credits for Businesses

Here are some of the most common and valuable tax credits that small and medium businesses should have on their radar:

- **Work Opportunity Tax Credit (WOTC):** This federal credit rewards businesses for hiring people from certain groups that face employment barriers (for example, veterans, people on long-term unemployment, or recipients of public assistance). The credit ranges from about $1,200 up to $9,600 per eligible hire, depending on the employee's category. For instance, if you hire a qualified veteran, you might get a $5,000 credit against your taxes. Not only do you gain a dedicated employee, but the government thanks you for it with a lower tax bill. In fact, collectively, businesses claim over $1 billion in WOTC credits each year, which shows how impactful this program is.

- **Research & Development (R&D) Tax Credit:** This credit is designed to spur innovation. If your company is investing in creating new products, improving processes, writing software, or any kind of technological development, you might be eligible. And it's not just for big tech firms or labs, small businesses in many industries can qualify. The R&D credit essentially let you recoup a portion of your R&D expenses by cutting your taxes. For example, a small manufacturing business that spends $50,000 on developing a new product prototype could potentially get a credit of several thousand dollars, easing the financial burden of innovation. Even startups that aren't yet profitable can benefit. Under current law, qualifying new businesses can apply up to $500,000 of R&D credits per year toward their payroll taxes (thanks to recent enhancements in the law).

- **Energy Investment Tax Credit (Solar ITC) and Other "Green" Credits:** If your business invests in renewable energy or energy-efficient equipment, you can get significant credits. The Solar Investment Tax Credit, for instance, currently allows a business to claim 30% of the cost of a solar installation as a direct credit. So, if you spend $20,000 on solar panels for your office, you could get a $6,000 credit back. There are also credits for other renewable technologies, and deductions or credits for making buildings more energy efficient. Not only do these upgrades lower your utility bills, but they also come with tax perks. Governments want businesses to go green and will literally pay you to do it via tax incentives.

- **Small Business Health Care Tax Credit:** Do you offer health insurance to your employees? If you have fewer than 25 full-time employees with average wages below a certain threshold, and you cover at least 50% of their premiums, you could qualify for this credit. It can be worth up to 50% of the premiums you pay, which is a huge help for a small company. For example, if you paid $40,000 in employee health premiums this year, the credit could be as much as $20,000 back to you for doing right by your team.

- **Local and State Incentives:** Beyond federal credits, many states and municipalities offer tax breaks to attract and grow businesses. These might include credits for creating jobs in certain areas (e.g., an urban redevelopment zone or rural area that needs investment), credits for offering training programs, or even grants and abatements for expanding your facilities. While these vary widely by location, it's worth checking your state's economic development website or talking to a local business development officer to see what's available. Some entrepreneurs are surprised to find incentives like a $5,000 credit for each new job they create in their city, or a property tax abatement for making improvements to an old building downtown.

Real-World Illustrations: Let's look at a couple of brief examples to see these credits in action.

- **Tech Startup Example:** iBrightTech Co., a small software startup, invested heavily in developing a new app. They spent $100,000 on developer salaries and cloud services specifically for this R&D project. Their accountant helped them calculate an R&D tax credit of about $10,000, which they applied to their payroll taxes (since they had no income tax liability yet). That $10,000 was money saved, enabling them to hire a part-time marketing assistant to launch the app. The credit literally turned into another employee for their team!

- **Hiring Credit Example:** Local Cafe & Bakery expanded this year and hired 10 new employees, two of whom were long-term unemployed individuals eager for a second chance. The owner made sure to file the WOTC paperwork for those two new hires. As a result, the cafe earned about $4,800 in WOTC credits. That covered a significant portion of their year-end tax bill. Essentially, the government helped pay for the cafe to grow its team and give jobs to those who needed them which resulted in a truly win-win situation.

- **Going Green Example:** Alexis, a salon owner, decided to replace her old water heaters with energy-efficient models and install a small solar panel system on the roof to help power her operations. The total project cost $15,000. She qualified for a 30% federal solar credit (approximately $4,500 off her taxes) and even got a smaller $1,000 rebate from her state energy department. On top of that, her monthly utility bills dropped by about 20%. By tapping into these incentives, Alexis recouped a large part of her investment within the first year and increased her salon's profit in the years after due to lower expenses.

How to Find Applicable Credits

Staying informed is key. Tax law changes, and new credits come and go (for example, the Employee Retention Credit (ERC) was a temporary credit that helped businesses keep employees during the COVID-19 pandemic).

To find current credits:

1. **Consult the IRS and Official Sources:** The IRS website (irs.gov) has a section on business credits and deductions. IRS Form 3800 (General Business Credit) instructions list many credits available for the tax year. These resources can be dense, but they're comprehensive.

2. **State and Local Resources:** Check your state's revenue department or economic development agency websites. They often have small business incentive guides. States like California, New York, Texas, etc., publish lists of credits for R&D, film production, job creation, etc.

3. **Professional Advice:** A tax professional or accountant who specializes in small business can be your scout. For instance, they will say, "Hey, you bought new equipment; there's a credit for that in this state." or "Did you know that you can get a credit for providing childcare for employees?" Don't hesitate to ask your CPA if there are any credits you might be missing.

4. **Industry Associations:** Many industry groups (like a manufacturing association, tech startup incubators, etc.) put out guides or host webinars on relevant incentives. If you're part of any business networks or associations, tap into that knowledge base.

By understanding what tax credits and incentives exist, you put yourself in a position to capture these opportunities rather than leave money on the table. Next, we will shift gears back to internal operations because maximizing profit isn't just about tax savings, but also about running your business efficiently and effectively. Let's explore how to boost your profits through smart business strategies in the following chapter.

Key Takeaways

Action Steps I Need to Takeaway

Questions to Ask My Consultant

Ideas for My Business Growth

Chapter 3

Strategies to Maximize Profitability

Overview
Maximizing your profits involves two sides of the equation: increasing revenue and decreasing costs. This chapter dives into practical strategies to do both, all while keeping an eye on how these decisions can interplay with tax benefits. Remember, profit maximization is an ongoing effort, and it's about creating a lean, smart business that generates more money than it spends, consistently.

Boost Your Revenue Streams
Growing your top line (sales) will obviously grow your profit, provided costs are kept in check.

Here are some ways to boost revenue:

Diversify Your Offerings
Consider if you can introduce new products or services that complement your current ones. For example, a graphic design freelancer might add website development services to serve clients more holistically (and increase income per client). An online retailer could introduce a subscription service for monthly curated products, adding steady recurring revenue.

Enhance Marketing and Sales Efforts
Are people aware of your business and its value? Invest in marketing that provides a clear return on investment. This could mean sharpening your social media strategy, starting an email newsletter, or improving your website's SEO to attract more customers. Sometimes a small investment in advertising can lead to a big jump in sales.

Increase Customer Value
It's often more cost effective to sell more to existing customers than to find new ones. Think about upsells or premium offerings. If you own a gym, can you offer personal training packages? If you run an e-commerce store, can you offer an extended warranty or faster shipping for a fee? Providing more value (at a profitable price) to customers who already trust you is a recipe for higher revenue.

Leverage Your Unique Strengths
Identify what makes your business special and double down on it. If you have exceptional customer service, highlight that, and perhaps charge a premium for a "white glove" version of your service. If you have a highly convenient location or superior technology, ensure your pricing reflects that added value.

Real-World Example – Revenue Growth: Consider Sophia's Gluten-Free Bakery.
She started with just custom cakes but after seeing how repeat customers often asked for bread and cookies, she expanded her menu. She also began selling baking mixes online nationwide. These new revenue streams doubled her sales in a year. Importantly, Sophia kept an eye on profitability. She priced the new items to ensure a good margin and was able to claim the

Domestic Production Activities Deduction (a now-phased-out federal incentive for products made in the USA) for her baking mixes while it lasted. By aligning her expansion with a tax incentive (manufacturing domestically), she saved on taxes while growing sales.

Control and Reduce Costs

The other side of profit is managing expenses. Every dollar you save is a dollar added to profit (and it might even reduce your taxes too!).

Here's how to cut costs smartly:

- **Conduct Regular Expense Audits:** At least twice a year, go through your expenses line by line. You will almost always find something that can be reduced or eliminated. Maybe it's a software subscription you don't use, or a phone plan that could be downgraded. Perhaps you're paying overtime when a part-time hire could be more cost-effective. Treat it like a game and challenge yourself to cut 5-10% off a major expense category without harming your business.

- **Negotiate with Suppliers:** Many vendors are willing to give discounts for bulk orders, early payments, or long-term relationships. If you've been a loyal customer to a supplier, ask for a better rate or shop around for a more competitive offer and give your current supplier a chance to match it. For example, a boutique owner renegotiated credit card processing fees and saved hundreds of dollars a month just by asking for a better rate due to her steady volume.

- **Optimize Operations:** Look for inefficiencies in how work gets done. Are you or your team spending hours on tasks that could be automated with affordable technology? For instance, switching to an online bookkeeping software might save you 10 hours of manual data entry each month, which you can then spend on sales or product development. A manufacturing business might invest in a piece of equipment that streamlines production because less labor time per unit produced means lower cost per unit (and possibly a Section 179 deduction or bonus depreciation on that equipment purchase, reducing taxes).

- **Control Overhead:** Keep a close eye on fixed costs like rent, utilities, and salaries. If you have unused office space, consider subleasing it. If your energy bills are high, upgrading to energy-efficient lighting or equipment could save money and might qualify for energy credits or deductions (as discussed in Chapter 2). If certain operations can be done remotely, you might even downsize to a smaller physical space.

- **Outsource or Automate Low-Value Tasks:** Identify tasks that are important but don't necessarily need to be done in-house. Accounting, payroll, IT support, or even marketing can often be outsourced to specialized firms or automated with software. This can sometimes be cheaper than maintaining full-time staff for those functions, especially for a small business. Plus, outsourcing gives you flexibility to scale services up or down as needed.

Real-World Example – Cost Cutting

Look at GreenTech Innovations (from a case study in Chapter 2) which struggled with tax compliance workload. They implemented a cloud-based tax management software, which not only ensured they never missed a tax deadline, but also reduced manual effort. This is a good example where a small investment in technology saved money indirectly by freeing up employee time to focus on revenue-generating activities. Another example is a restaurant that installed smart energy monitors and discovered their ovens ran all night by mistake, wasting electricity. Fixing that issue and training staff to shut down equipment properly saved them $4,000 in annual utility costs straight to the bottom line.

Integrate Tax Strategy into Business Strategy
A truly savvy entrepreneur thinks about taxes throughout the year, not just at tax time. This doesn't mean making decisions solely for tax reasons (you should never spend a dollar just to save 30 cents in tax), but it means being aware of the tax impact of your business decisions.

Choose the Right Business Structure
As your business grows, the structure (sole proprietor, LLC, S-Corp, C-Corp, etc.) can significantly affect how much tax you pay. For instance, as an S-Corporation, you might save on self-employment taxes by paying yourself a reasonable salary and taking remaining profits as distributions. Changing from a sole proprietorship to an LLC or corporation can also offer other tax benefits and liability protection. Always consult a professional when considering a reorganization but know that structure matters for taxes.

Plan Major Purchases with Tax in Mind
If you know you need to buy a big piece of equipment or invest in a vehicle for your business, timing can impact your taxes. Buying and placing an asset into service before year end might allow you to take a depreciation deduction or credit this year rather than next. On the flip side, if you're already having a low profit year (and thus low tax), you might decide to wait on a purchase until a year when your profit (and tax) will be higher, so the deduction is more valuable. The key is planning rather than impulsively spending.

Employment and Tax Credits
When you are hiring or expanding your team, remember the credits we discussed. Include in your HR process to check for WOTC eligibility for new hires. It might slightly tweak who you consider for a role (for example, giving an opportunity to someone who has been unemployed for a long time can both help them and earn you a credit). Similarly, if you're embarking on a project that could qualify for R&D credits, set up a system from the start to track those expenses separately. That way, come tax time, you have the documentation ready to claim the credit.

State and Local Tax Strategy
If your business operates in multiple states or could, be mindful of the different tax rates and incentives. A company expanding online sales might choose to warehouse products in a state with no sales tax to consumers or lower corporate taxes to optimize overall profitability. (Just ensure compliance with all state laws. Multi-state taxation can be complex, but savings can be material for the right business.)

Continuous Learning
Tax laws and business environments change. For example, a few years back, no one knew the pandemic would bring about the Employee Retention Credit or special SBA subsidies. By staying informed through your CPA, news, or industry workshops you can adapt quickly. One business owner regularly attends an annual tax update seminar for entrepreneurs; the one-time fee for the workshop often pays for itself multiple times over in new savings discovered. Staying educated ensures you don't miss out on new opportunities or get caught off guard by new regulations.

Real-World Example: Holistic Strategy

Think of Nora, who runs a small but growing online craft supplies store. Early on, she realized that if she kept doing everything herself, she would burn out and the business would stall. She hired two employees. Knowing about WOTC, she made one of those hires a military spouse (a group that can qualify the business for a tax credit because military families often face employment hurdles). Nora got a $2,400 tax credit for that hire. She also switched from a sole proprietorship to an S-Corp when her profits became substantial, saving about $5,000 a year in taxes by reducing self-employment tax on part of her earnings. These decisions required planning and advice, but they directly increased her net profits.

Nora's story underlines a key point: profitability isn't just about making more and spending less, it's also about smart tax planning every step of the way.

Monitoring and Metrics
You can't improve what you don't measure. Profitable businesses often have strong financial habits.

- **Use a Budget:** Create a budget for your business each year (or even each quarter) that includes projected revenues and planned expenses. Track your actual numbers against it. This will highlight areas where you're overspending or undershooting on sales so you can course-correct quickly.

- **Key Performance Indicators (KPIs):** Identify a few KPIs that drive your profitability. For example, This could be your gross profit margin, customer acquisition cost, average transaction value, or labor as a percentage of sales. Review these regularly and if a KPI is moving in the wrong direction, dig in to understand why.

- **Regular Financial Reviews:** As mentioned in Chapter 1, set aside time to review financial performance. This includes looking at your P&L (profit and loss statement) and cash flow. Understanding your financial statements is empowering. If something is off and you catch it early, small adjustments can prevent big problems. Conversely, if you notice a positive trend (say, a product line is very high margin), you can focus more on that area.

Action Steps – Boosting Profitability

- **Implement One Revenue Booster:** Choose one idea to increase revenue (a new product, a marketing push, a partnership, etc.) and create a simple plan to execute it in the next quarter.

- **Trim One Expense Category:** Identify one expense category (marketing, utilities, subscriptions, etc.) to reduce by at least 10% without harming your business. Brainstorm how to achieve that and take action this month.

- **Tax-Smart Planning:** Make a checklist of the tax-related strategies you want to pursue (e.g., look into changing the business entity, research local incentives for hiring, set up an R&D tracking sheet). Schedule time with your tax advisor or do research on the top item on your list.

- **Set Up Tracking:** If you don't have a bookkeeping system, start using one (even a simple spreadsheet can work if you're very small, though software is better). Ensure you're categorizing expenses and maybe tag any potentially credit-eligible expenses (like R&D costs) separately for ease at tax time.

By proactively increasing your revenues and prudently managing your costs, you set the stage for a healthy profit. Now, with your business running more efficiently and profitably, it's time to focus on capturing those tax credits and ensuring you meet all requirements to actually get the money. In the next chapter, we'll walk through how to qualify for and claim the credits that can further boost your bottom line.

Key Takeaways

Action Steps I Need to Takeaway

Questions to Ask My Consultant

Ideas for My Business Growth

Chapter 4

Qualifying for and Claiming Tax Credits

By now, you understand how valuable tax credits can be and which ones are out there. However, knowledge alone doesn't save money, you have to take action to actually secure those credits. In this chapter, we'll guide you through the process of determining your eligibility and successfully claiming tax credits for your business. It's like a treasure hunt: we know the treasure (credits) is there, now we need the map and tools to dig it up.

1. **Know the Rules and Criteria: Each tax credit comes with its own set of rules. To claim the credit, you must meet these requirements to the letter. Here's how to get started:**

   - **Research the Credit Requirements:** For any credit you're aiming to claim, find the official criteria. For example, to claim the Work Opportunity Tax Credit (WOTC), you must hire someone from one of the specified target groups and obtain certification from your state's workforce agency within 28 days of the employee's start date. If you miss that window, you lose the credit. Likewise, the R&D Credit requires that the nature of your research activities meets the IRS's definitions (they have a four-part test for what counts as qualified research) and that you have records of the expenses. Make a checklist for each credit of the exact conditions that must be met.

   - **Use Official Forms and Instructions:** The IRS and other agencies provide forms to claim credits. Some common ones are:

     - ✓ IRS Form 5884 for WOTC
     - ✓ Form 6765 for R&D Credit
     - ✓ Form 3468 for investment credits like solar, and
     - ✓ Form 8941 for the Small Business Health Care Credit.

     These usually come with instructions that detail the qualification criteria. Don't be intimidated by the forms often the first step is just reading through them to get a clearer picture of what information is needed. If it looks overwhelming, that's a sign you might benefit from professional help (more on that soon).

   - **Mind Your Documentation:** If you think you might qualify for a credit, start documenting everything related to it. As mentioned, for a hiring credit like WOTC, you need that certification, so your documentation is the approval from the state (keep copies!). For an R&D credit, documentation includes project notes, invoices for supplies, payroll records showing which employees worked on R&D and how much of their time, etc. For an energy credit, save receipts, contracts, and any manufacturer certification that qualifies the equipment. Basically, if you were ever audited, you want a neat folder that clearly shows you met all the credit's requirements and how you calculated the amount.

2. **Get Professional Help (if needed):** Tax credits can be one of the trickiest parts of tax prep. Many entrepreneurs find it well worth it to work with a Certified Public Accountant (CPA) or tax advisor, at least for the first time they claim a new credit. A professional can help:

    - **Identify Credits:** Sometimes you might not even realize you qualify for a credit until a pro points it out. For example, many small businesses didn't know about the Employee Retention Credit until their accountant mentioned it in 2021. A good tax advisor stays updated on these programs.

    - **File Correctly:** They can handle the forms and ensure everything is filled out properly. The CPA hired for a bakery client not only got them caught up on deductions, but also identified a credit for hiring that they qualified for. The CPA navigated the paperwork and the bakery received significant tax savings. Accountants also often have software that flags potential credits based on your financial data.

    - **Strategize Timing:** Pros can advise on the timing of actions. Maybe it's worth accelerating a planned expense into this year to qualify for a credit that's expiring, or deferring something to next year when a new credit kicks in.

    - **Handle Complex Calculations:** Some credits (like R&D) involve complex calculations or choosing between methods of calculation. Having an expert ensure you're getting the maximum benefit is helpful.

    - If hiring a CPA is not feasible, you might consider tax preparation software which often has question prompts about credits (though software might not catch everything). At minimum, do some research or consult free resources (the IRS sometimes offers helplines or FAQs for specific credits).

3. **Step-by-Step: Claiming a Credit:** While each credit differs, here is a generalized step-by-step approach when you decide to go for a particular credit:

    - **Confirm Eligibility:** Double-check to see if you meet all the criteria before you count on the credit. (E.g., did you really spend money in the right categories? Does the activity date fall in the correct tax year? Is the person you hired definitely eligible for WOTC? etc.)

    - **Fill Out the Specific Credit Form:** Complete the IRS form (or equivalent state form) for that credit. For example, if you're claiming the R&D credit, fill out Form 6765 with all the required info about your research expenses.

    - **Include it in Your Tax Return:** Most business credits for federal taxes ultimately get tallied on Form 3800 (General Business Credit) which then flows into your main tax return. If you use a tax preparer or software, they will handle this flow. Essentially, you list all your individual credits, and they sum it up to offset your tax liability.

- **Attach/Submit Required Documentation:** Some credits require you to attach certification or proof when you file; others you just keep records in case of audit. For WOTC, you need to have the certification letter for each employee from the state these aren't sent to the IRS with your return, but you must have them on file. For a credit like a state tax credit, you might need to include a copy of the state's approval form with your state tax return. Always read the form instructions to know what's required.

- **Carryovers:** If the credit is bigger than your tax bill and it's not refundable, most credits allow you to carry unused amounts forward to future years. Keep track of any carryforward. For instance, if you had a $50,000 R&D credit but could only use $30,000 this year due to your tax amount, you likely can carry the remaining $20,000 to next year's taxes. Don't forget about it!

- **Amend if Necessary:** If you discover a credit after you already filed taxes for a year, you can often go back and amend that return (within the amendment window, generally 3 years for federal taxes) to claim it. This can get you a refund check. It's a bit of extra paperwork, but it can be worth it if the credit is substantial.

4. Avoid Common Pitfalls

- **Missing Deadlines:** Some credits have application deadlines. Apart from WOTC's 28-day rule, consider state credits that might require you to apply before year-end or even pre-approval before you do the activity. Mark your calendar for any key dates.

- **Assuming You Don't Qualify:** Many business owners mistakenly think credits are for "other companies, not me." Don't assume, check. Even if your business is small, you might be surprised. For example, a two-person startup could get an R&D credit; a five-employee retail shop could get a credit for providing access for disabled customers (the Disabled Access Credit) if they spent money on a ramp or ADA-compliant restroom.

- **Lack of Documentation:** We mentioned this but it's worth repeating: if you ever get audited, the IRS will ask for proof. No receipts, no credit. Keep a credit file for each year where you put any relevant documents for any credit you plan to claim.

- **Not Amending Returns:** If you find out about a credit later, don't just say "oh well, missed that." If it's within the allowed time, amend your return and get that money. I've seen businesses receive tens of thousands in refunds for prior years because they went back and claimed credits, they were entitled to but overlooked initially.

- **Over reliance on Credits:** While credits are fantastic, don't let the "tax tail wag the dog." Make business decisions for business reasons first. For instance, don't hire someone unneeded just for a WOTC credit. That credit is a one-time benefit and far smaller than a year's wages. Instead, use the credit to amplify good decisions you were going to make anyway (hiring a great candidate who happens to qualify, investing in equipment you need, etc.). Credits should enhance, not drive, your strategy.

5. Case Study – Claiming Credits in Practice: Let's walk through a hypothetical scenario combining a couple of credits:

Scenario: Maria runs a small tech company with 10 employees. In 2025, she undertook a project to develop a new software tool (R&D credit potential) and also hired two new employees, one of whom is a qualified veteran (WOTC potential).

What Maria Did: Early in the year, she learned about the R&D credit. She set up a project code in her accounting system for all expenses related to the new software tool. All of the hours her developers spent on this project were tracked, and all cloud service bills and contractor invoices were tagged. When tax time came, she had spent $80,000 on the project. She worked with her CPA, who calculated the federal R&D credit at roughly $8,000. Meanwhile, for the new veteran hire, Maria's HR manager ensured the WOTC application was submitted within a couple of weeks of hire. They received certification that this employee qualified for a $5,600 credit (based on the veteran's prior length of unemployment). Maria's CPA filled out the forms for both credits. Maria ended up owing almost no federal tax for 2025 because those credits offset most of her liability. She kept the certification letter and R&D documentation on file, just in case. Essentially, she turned diligent planning and paperwork into real dollars of savings.

Result: The $13,600 saved in taxes was used to buy new laptops for her team and boost the company's marketing budget for 2026, fueling further growth.

Action Steps – Start Claiming Your Credits

- **Make a Credits List:** Write down three tax credits that you think your business could potentially qualify for (use Chapters 2 and 3 for ideas). For each, note the key eligibility requirements.

- **Choose One to Pursue Now:** Pick the credit that seems most accessible for you at this moment. Take the first step: download the IRS form or official guidance for that credit and identify what information you need. If it's a hiring credit, coordinate with your HR (or if you are HR, set aside time to handle the paperwork) to start the process.

- **Get Help if Stuck:** If after looking at the forms you're feeling lost, schedule an hour with a tax consultant or reach out to a local Small Business Development Center. Sometimes a quick consultation can clarify a lot.

- **Mark Your Calendar:** If your chosen credit has a deadline (like our WOTC example or a state incentive application), put a reminder on your calendar a few weeks before that deadline so you don't miss it.

- **Organize Your Documents:** Create a digital or physical folder labeled "Tax Credits – [Year]". Whenever you do something that might earn a credit (hire someone, spend on R&D, buy equipment), drop the supporting documents in that folder immediately. When it's tax time, you won't be scrambling to find proof; it'll be ready to go.

Claiming tax credits might seem bureaucratic, but it's a high-impact activity for your bottom line. With this knowledge and preparation, you are turning into the kind of entrepreneur who doesn't leave free money on the table. In the next chapter, we'll pull everything together mindset, profitability, and tax strategy so you can move forward confidently on your journey to business success.

Key Takeaways

Action Steps I Need to Takeaway

Questions to Ask My Consultant

Ideas for My Business Growth

Chapter 5

Putting It All Together – Profits, Growth, and Beyond

Overview

You've laid the foundation with a profit-first mindset, learned about powerful tax credits, optimized your business operations, and navigated the process of claiming credits. Now it's time to bring it all together. Let's discuss how to maintain this momentum, adapt to future changes, and continue building a business that is both profitable and resilient.

The Synergy of Strategy and Savings: By now, you can see how each piece of the puzzle connects.

- ✓ Focusing on profit ensures your business is healthy and sustainable.

- ✓ Efficient operations and cost management free up resources (cash and time) that can be reinvested or saved.

- ✓ Tax credits and smart tax planning provide boosts to your profit by cutting down one of your largest expenses (taxes).

Reinvesting those saved dollars back into the business whether through marketing, hiring, or innovation creates a cycle of growth.

Think of this approach as running your business with the full toolkit. You're not just grinding away hoping money will show up; you're deliberately using every tool at your disposal (strategy, finance & tax laws) to make sure your business prospers. This comprehensive approach is what separates struggling businesses from thriving ones.

Stay Agile and Informed: The business landscape and tax laws will continue to evolve. As an entrepreneur dedicated to maximizing profit, you should plan to stay informed and agile.

- **Keep Learning:** Make it a habit to update your knowledge. Tax laws can change with new government policies. For instance, a new administration might introduce a credit for hiring apprentices or change the percentage on the solar credit. By subscribing to a quality newsletter or checking in with your accountant annually about "what's new this year?", you'll be ahead of the curve. Remember the example of the consultancy firm that invested in training their team annually to keep up with tax changes as a small business owner, you might not need formal seminars, but you can certainly devote a bit of time to educate yourself each year.

- **Monitor Your Industry and Community:** Sometimes industry-specific incentives pop up. If you're in manufacturing, keep an eye on legislation around manufacturing credits. If you're in tech, watch for tech startup incentives or grants. Local governments often roll out time-limited programs (for example, a city might waive certain fees or give a tax credit for businesses that open in a certain neighborhood within the next two years). By staying plugged into your local business community (through chambers of commerce, local business news, etc.), you can capitalize on these opportunities.

- **Plan for the Long Term:** Consider creating a 5-year financial plan for your business that includes both growth and tax strategies. Where do you want your revenue and profit to be in a few years? How will you get there? Identify investments you'll need to make (like new equipment, more employees, maybe a new location or product line) and research what incentives might help with those when the time comes. For example, if you know in two years you'll want to develop a new product, remember to budget for R&D and plan to use the R&D credit. If you're thinking about getting a building, look into any credits for historic building rehabilitation or energy-efficient construction.

- **Build a Strong Advisory Network:** You don't have to do this alone. Surround yourself with a few key advisors. We've talked about accountants a lot but also consider mentors or a mastermind group of fellow entrepreneurs where you share tips and hold each other accountable. Maybe you have a lawyer, a financial planner, or a business coach you check in with. When you have people you trust to bounce ideas off, you'll make more informed decisions. They might alert you to something like, "Hey, have you heard about the new credit for XYZ? You should look into it."

- **Stay Compliant and Ethical:** As you push to maximize profits and minimize taxes, always remember to keep things above board. The goal is to take advantage of legal incentives, not to bend rules. If something seems too good to be true or is a "gray area", get professional advice or err on the side of caution. The last thing you want after all this progress is a setback due to penalties or legal issues. The good news is everything we've focused on from cutting unnecessary costs to claiming legitimate credits is fully within the rules and intent of the law.

Real-World Inspiration – A Success Story
Let's revisit our fictional friend Jackson & Sons Manufacturing a couple of years later. After their initial turnaround (from Chapter 1's example), they didn't stop there. The owners continued to review their profit margins regularly, finding new ways to be efficient. They implemented an employee suggestion program that rewarded ideas for saving money. This boosted engagement and cut costs even more when good ideas were put in place.

They also kept using tax credits: every new hire was evaluated for WOTC, and when they decided to develop a new eco-friendly product line, they tapped an R&D credit and even a state green manufacturing credit. They also started attending an annual tax incentive workshop to stay on top of new opportunities. Fast forward, Jackson & Sons grew its profit by 150% over three years. They expanded to a new facility and increased staff by 30%, essentially funding their expansion through the profits and tax savings they diligently captured. The owners now mentor other local businesses, showing that when you run your business wisely and take advantage of available resources, even a once-struggling company can become a pillar of the community.

As we close Chapter 5 on the power of unlocking tax credits, it's important to remember that maximizing profits goes far beyond deductions it's about designing a business that takes care of YOU.

Now that you understand how to retain more of your money through strategic credits, let's take it a step further. What if your business didn't just reduce your taxes but actually paid for your health care, your vehicle, your education, even your vacations?

The next chapter will help you move from reactive savings to proactive financial engineering. It's time to learn how to fully utilize your business to benefit your personal lifestyle, all while staying compliant, building wealth, and keeping more of what you earn.

Let's dive into Chapter 6 and make your business work for you and not the other way around.

Key Takeaways

Action Steps I Need to Takeaway

Questions to Ask My Consultant

Ideas for My Business Growth

Chapter 6

How to Use Your Business to Benefit YOU

Many entrepreneurs fail to realize that their business is not just a source of income but also a powerful tool for building a better life. The IRS allows a wide array of personal expenses to be converted into legal, tax-deductible business expenses, as long as they are ordinary and necessary. This chapter will walk you through how to set your business up to work for YOU.

Detailed Concepts

- Home Office Deduction: Allocate a portion of your rent/mortgage, utilities, and internet if used for business.

- Vehicle Use: Business vehicles can be written off using actual expenses or standard mileage.

- Business Travel: Turn conferences, retreats, or client meetings in attractive locations into deductions.

- Professional Development: Courses, certifications, books, and seminars can be classified as business expenses.

- Hiring Family: Employ your spouse or children and offer benefits like healthcare or retirement contributions.

Real Life Example

Melanie, a business strategist, restructured her consulting firm to include her home office as a deductible space. She took a business trip to San Diego for a conference that also included leisure activities, saving thousands by making the trip 80% tax deductible.

Making Your Business Work for YOU

This flowchart illustrates how strategic financial planning within your business can lead to powerful personal and financial outcomes.

1. Revenue

    - All income generated through products, services, or contracts.
    - Example: $100,000 in gross revenue from coaching, consulting, or product sales.

2. Business Expenses

    - Legitimate, tax-deductible costs related to operating the business.
    - Examples: office rent, staff wages, software, marketing, travel, training.

3. Owner Benefits

    - Business covers expenses that also benefit the owner personally, legally.
    - Examples: vehicle lease, home office, health insurance, phone, meals.

4. Tax Deductions

    - These business expenses reduce taxable income, saving you money.
    - Example: Instead of paying taxes on $100K, you're taxed on $45K.

5. Reinvested Profits

    - Use tax savings and leftover profits to reinvest in growth, pay yourself, or create new income streams.
    - Examples: retirement accounts, business expansion, team hires, passive income assets.

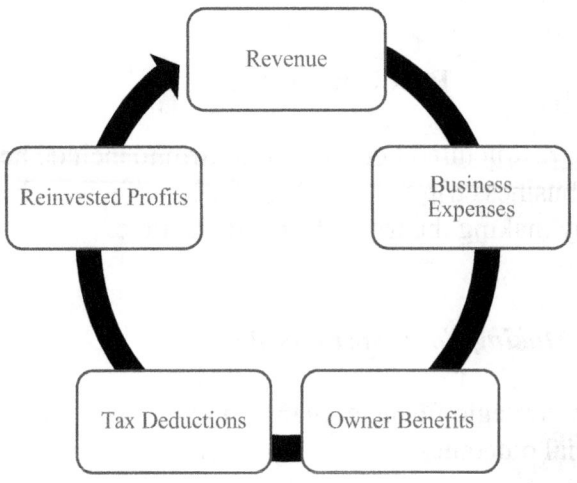

Action Step:

List three personal expenses you currently pay out-of-pocket. How can they be transitioned into your business?

1. _____

2. _____

3. _____

Take Action:

1. Create a business expense checklist.

2. Consult a tax advisor to legitimize new deductions.

3. Start tracking and categorizing your expenses monthly.

What are you thinking?

_____

_____

_____

_____

_____

_____

_____

_____

Key Takeaways

Action Steps I Need to Takeaway

Questions to Ask My Consultant

Ideas for My Business Growth

Chapter 7

Creating a Legacy – So Your Business Doesn't Stop With You

Overview

A true entrepreneur builds something that outlives them. Legacy planning through your business means preparing your children, team, and succession plan to carry the vision forward.

Legacy Builders Checklist:

- ✓ Create a living trust or will with business inclusion.
- ✓ Teach your children or successors financial literacy.
- ✓ Develop SOPs (Standard Operating Procedures).
- ✓ Appoint a successor or build a board of advisors.

Example:

Grace Anchored Inc. was designed with a legacy in mind. Melanie is training others to run the nonprofit using a blueprint so that it serves communities even in her absence.

Action Step:

Create a one-page vision for your business legacy. Who will lead it in your absence? What core values must remain?

CHAPTER 8:

Offering Services That YOU Need: Health, Vision, Dental, Retirement, & More

Overview
Your business can become your benefits provider. With the right structure, it can pay for:

- ✓ Health Insurance
- ✓ Vision & Dental care
- ✓ HSA or FSA accounts
- ✓ Retirement Plans (SEP IRA, Solo 401(k))
- ✓ Childcare Assistance

Practical Tip: Use a Section 105 Plan or hire your spouse or children to offer benefits legally and get the tax deductions.

Example: Melanie hired her daughter part-time and offered health benefits through the company. The premiums and out-of-pocket medical expenses were deducted pre-tax.

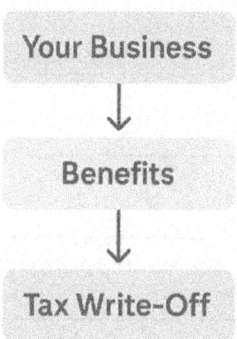

Checklist:

- ✓ Get a business EIN and bank account.
- ✓ Choose a benefits provider.
- ✓ Document employee benefits properly.

Key Takeaways

Action Steps I Need to Takeaway

Questions to Ask My Consultant

Ideas for My Business Growth

CHAPTER 9

Position Your Business for Global Reach

Overview

The internet leveled the playing field. Your business can now serve clients in Dubai, Lagos, London, or Brazil with a few clicks.

Steps to Go Global:

1. Register a website with international SEO.

2. Accept global payments (Stripe, Payoneer, Wise).

3. Set up legal international contracts.

4. Understand import/export rules (if product-based).

5. Consider translation/localization of services.

Example:

Empowered Dominion Network now offers online courses to clients in the U.S., Africa, and the Caribbean. It uses Zoom + Kajabi + PayPal with multi-currency acceptance.

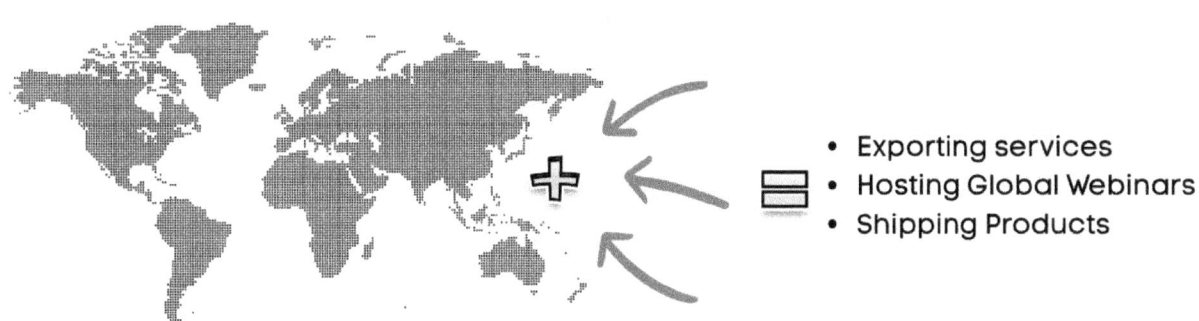

Action Step:

Identify 2 countries you could serve. Write a brief marketing pitch tailored to that audience.

Key Takeaways

Action Steps I Need to Takeaway

Questions to Ask My Consultant

Ideas for My Business Growth

CHAPTER 10

Create a Strong, Self-Sustaining Network

Overview

Your net worth is often linked to your network. Building a community around your brand can:

- ✓ Increase referrals.
- ✓ Attract investors.
- ✓ Build trust and brand value.
- ✓ Scale your message and mission.

Types of Networks to Build:

- ✓ Peer network (other CEOs)
- ✓ Team network (mentors, consultants, vendors)
- ✓ Client community (loyal buyers, members)

Example:

Empowered Dominion Network built a Facebook group + monthly Zoom mixers + affiliate program. As a result, EDN clients support and refer each other.

Notes Section:

1. Who are your top 5 connections that could help you grow?
2. What event or platform can you use to bring your network together?

Key Takeaways

Action Steps I Need to Takeaway

Questions to Ask My Consultant

Ideas for My Business Growth

Final Thoughts

You're Not Just in Business You're Building a Movement

The journey you've taken through this book is more than just financial it's foundational. As a visionary entrepreneur, you aren't simply running a company; you're shifting culture, creating jobs, and leaving a legacy. You've learned how to structure your business, maximize profits, unlock tax advantages, and position your venture for long-term growth. But more importantly, you've started a movement: a mission-driven business that reflects your values and creates impact.

Keep building. Stay compliant. Innovate boldly. And remember your business isn't just about income, it's about influence. Let your light shine and inspire others to do the same.

-Melanie

Bonus: Checklists and Resources

To help you implement what you've learned, use the following checklists and resources as practical tools. These will keep you on track in maximizing profits and ensuring you don't miss out on valuable tax credits.

- ✓ Profit Maximization Checklist
- ✓ Tax Credit Eligibility Checklist
- ✓ Business Expense Tracking Sheet
- ✓ Annual Profit Planner Template
- ✓ Business Legacy Vision Worksheet
- ✓ Global Expansion Readiness Questionnaire
- ✓ Self-Sustaining Network Builder Template

Profit Maximization Checklist

Pricing for Profit
- Have you reviewed your pricing in the last year to ensure it covers all costs and includes a healthy margin?
- Tip: Use cost-plus pricing or value-based pricing to set the right price.

Expense Audit
- Did you conduct an expense audit this quarter?
- List at least three expenses to reduce or eliminate. (e.g., cancel unused subscriptions, renegotiate a vendor contract, reduce energy usage).

Budget vs. Actual
- Do you compare your monthly financial results against your budget?
- Note any big variances and investigate the causes (for instance, if marketing expenses were $500 over budget, was it planned or did costs spike unexpectedly?).

Cash Flow Management
- Are you managing cash flow proactively?
- Check if you have a cash buffer (savings) for at least 2-3 months of expenses, and if you're invoicing promptly/collecting receivables on time.

Invest in Growth (Wisely):
- Identify one area where a small investment could yield higher revenue or lower costs.
- Did you set aside profit to reinvest in this opportunity? (e.g., upgrading to a more efficient machine, training an employee to improve skills, launching a targeted ad campaign).

Profit Review Meeting:
- Did you schedule your regular "profit review" meeting? (Even if it's a solo review, put it on your calendar monthly or quarterly to evaluate profitability and set actions for improvement).

Tax Credits Eligibility Checklist

- **Work Opportunity Tax Credit (WOTC):** Did you hire any new employees from target groups (veterans, long-term unemployed, recipients of certain assistance programs, etc.)? If yes, did you submit the required form to your state workforce agency within 28 days of hire for each eligible employee?

- **Research & Development (R&D) Credit:** Are you developing new products, processes, or software in your business? If yes, are you tracking those project expenses (wages, materials, contractor costs) separately? Make sure to document project details to support qualifying R&D activities.

- **Energy Investment Tax Credit (Solar or Renewable Energy):** Have you invested in solar panels, solar water heating, or other renewable energy property for your business? If so, save all receipts and manufacturer certifications you can likely claim 30% of those costs as a federal tax credit. Also, check for state or utility rebates.

- **Small Business Health Care Tax Credit:** Do you provide health insurance to your employees? If you have fewer than 25 full-time equivalent employees with average wages under the limit and you cover at least 50% of their premiums, ensure you calculate this credit. (Typically, you must purchase coverage through the SHOP Marketplace to qualify, if applicable).

- **State/Local Credits:** Did you research at least one state or local incentive? (For example, credits for creating jobs, investing in certain equipment, or locating your business in a specific zone). Note down any program and check the application process.

- **Disabled Access Credit:** (If applicable) Did you spend money this year to make your business more accessible (installing ramps, modifying restrooms, etc.) for disabled individuals? If yes, look into the Disabled Access Credit, which can cover 50% of eligible expenses up to $5,000 credit.

- **Employee Retention/Other Special Credits:** If there were any special circumstances (like recovery from a natural disaster or a new temporary incentive program), did you check if you qualify? For instance, some regions have credits for businesses that rebuild after hurricanes or other local programs. Keep an ear out for news that might apply to you.

- **Documentation Check:** For each credit above that you plan to claim, do you have a folder (digital or physical) with all the required supporting documents (receipts, forms, notes, etc.)? If not, make a list of what you need to gather.

Business Expense Tracking Sheet

Business Name: _____   Month/Year: _____

Date	Expense Description	Category	Vendor	Payment Method	Amount	Receipt (Y/N)	Notes

Categories to include: Office Supplies, Rent/Utilities, Marketing/Advertising, Travel, Meals/Entertainment, Professional Fees, Salaries/Contractors, Miscellaneous

Monthly Total Expenses: _____

Prepared by: _____

Reviewed by: _____

Annual Profit Planner Template

Business Name: _____ Fiscal Year: _____

1. Revenue Forecast

Month	Expected Sales	Recurring Income	One-Time Income	Total Revenue

2. Planned Expenses

Expense Category	Monthly Average	Annual Total

3. Projected Profit

Annual Revenue: _____

Annual Expenses: _____

Projected Profit: _____

Key Goals for Profit Growth:

- _____

- _____

Business Legacy Vision Worksheet

Founder/Leader: _____   Date: _____

1. What legacy do you want your business to leave? _____
_____

2. Who will benefit from your legacy? _____
_____

3. What core values must be preserved? _____
_____

4. What systems will ensure sustainability? _____
_____

5. What actions must you take now? _____
_____

6. Legacy Milestones (1, 5, 10 years):

Timeline	Milestone	Responsible Person	Due Date

Global Expansion Readiness Questionnaire

Business Name: _____ Date: _____

1. Current Markets Served: _____

2. Desired Countries/Regions: _____

3. Have you conducted international market research? ☐ Yes ☐ No

4. Do you have the following in place?

Factor	Status	Notes
Legal compliance in target country	☐ Ready ☐ In Progress	
Local partnerships	☐ Ready ☐ In Progress	
Logistics & Supply Chain	☐ Ready ☐ In Progress	
Cross-cultural team	☐ Ready ☐ In Progress	
Multi-currency pricing	☐ Ready ☐ In Progress	
Translation/localization	☐ Ready ☐ In Progress	
Global marketing plan	☐ Ready ☐ In Progress	

5. Greatest Risks & Mitigation: _____

6. Expansion Timeline: _____

7. Global Vision Statement: _____

Self-Sustaining Network Builder Template

Network Name: _____   Coordinator: _____

1. Purpose of the Network:
_____

2. Who are your ideal partners/members?
_____

3. What value will each member contribute?
_____

Member Name	Contribution	Commitment Level	Next Steps

4. Revenue Streams to Sustain the Network:
- Membership Fees: _____
- Sponsorships: _____
- Joint Ventures: _____
- Other: _____

5. Communication & Collaboration Structure:
- Meetings: _____
- Tools/Platforms: _____

6. Roles & Responsibilities:

Role	Assigned To	Tasks	Review Date

7. Sustainability Plan:
- How will you ensure growth? _____
- How will you replace key people? _____
- How will you measure success? _____

Additional Resources

- **IRS Small Business Portal:** The IRS website's Small Business and Self-Employed section provides guides on deductions and credits, forms, and publications. (Recommended reading: IRS Publication 334, Tax Guide for Small Business, updated annually).

- **IRS Form 3800 Instructions:** A useful document to skim, as it lists all the general business credits for the year and references to specific forms for each credit.

- **Small Business Development Centers (SBDCs):** These centers (often associated with colleges or local economic agencies) provide free or low-cost consulting. They can often help you understand financial statements or point you toward tax credit resources in your area.

- **SCORE Mentors:** SCORE (Service Corps of Retired Executives) offers free mentoring by experienced business folks. A SCORE mentor can help you brainstorm profit strategies or just act as a sounding board for your plans.

Books and Blogs:

Profit First by Mike Michalowicz – A highly recommended read for developing a profit-first habit in your business finances.

Lower Your Taxes Big Time by Sandy Botkin – A book that, while focused on individuals and small businesses, shares strategies and tips to legally minimize taxes (including home office, meals, travel, and more).

Blogs like Entrepreneur.com, SmallBizTrends, or TaxAdvisor often have articles on new tax law changes or financial management tips. Set Google alerts or periodically search for topics like "small business tax credit 2025" to keep current.

Networking and Workshops: Join local chambers of commerce or industry groups. Many host workshops or luncheons on business topics. For example, a local chamber might have a CPA give a talk on year-end tax planning. These events can be gold mines for learning and making connections.

Tax Professionals: If your budget allows, establish a relationship with a CPA or Enrolled Agent who understands small businesses. Even one meeting a year for a consultation can help ensure you're not missing anything major. They can also review your prior returns for missed credits or deductions (and help file amendments if needed).

Keep this checklist and resource list handy. Update it with notes of your own. The more proactive you are in using these tools, the more you'll get out of them in dollars saved and confidence earned.

Notes

Use this space to jot down your ideas, action plans, or important takeaways as you work on your business. For example, note which credits you aim to pursue, key financial goals, or contacts of professionals who can help you. This is your personal section to reinforce what you've learned.

_____

_____

_____

_____

_____

_____

_____

_____

_____

_____

_____

_____

_____

_____

_____

Resources & References

The following resources were consulted and used to support the strategies, facts, and recommendations provided in this book:

Government & Regulatory Websites

Internal Revenue Service (IRS)
Website: www.irs.gov
Used for information on business structures, allowable deductions, tax credit programs, EIN registration, and compliance tips.

U.S. Small Business Administration (SBA)
Website: www.sba.gov
Used for business planning tools, funding resources, and business credit guidance.

SAM.gov (System for Award Management)
Website: www.sam.gov
Referenced for federal contract registration steps and eligibility.

Grants.gov
Website: www.grants.gov
For federal grant opportunities and application processes.

U.S. Department of the Treasury – Community Development Financial Institutions (CDFI) Fund
Website: www.cdfifund.gov
Referenced for funding and tax credit programs such as the New Markets Tax Credit.

Books & Industry Literature

Tax Savvy for Small Business **by Frederick W. Daily (Nolo Press)**
- Provides insights on legitimate tax deduction strategies.

Profit First **by Mike Michalowicz**
- A referenced method for cash flow management and prioritizing business profitability.

Business Development & Financial Education Tools

Empowered Dominion Network (EDN) – Internal Framework
- Proprietary tools and systems developed by Melanie E. Lewis to guide business owners through strategic planning, tax optimization, and financial empowerment.

EDN Tax Credit Maximizer™ Worksheet (Workbook Companion)
- Custom worksheet created to help readers apply the book's strategies in real time.

Digital Tools & Resources

IRS e-Services
Website: https://www.irs.gov/e-services
For tax professionals managing client records, PTINs, and EFINs.

Dun & Bradstreet (D-U-N-S Number)
Website: https://www.dnb.com
Referenced for business credit and supplier registration.

NAICS Codes Search Tool
Website: https://www.naics.com/search/
To ensure accurate industry classification for funding and tax purposes.

Interviews & Case Studies

Real-world examples, business case studies, and client scenarios shared with permission by small business owners and entrepreneurs who have worked with Melanie E. Lewis through iPhoenix Financial Tax Group and the Empowered Dominion Network (EDN).

Faith-Based Perspective

Holy Bible – King James Version (KJV)
- Used to provide faith-based encouragement and biblical foundations for kingdom entrepreneurship.

Your Journey Forward

Now it's your turn to put this information into practice in your own business. Remember, small steps consistently taken lead to big changes. The end of this book is really the beginning of a new approach to your business:

- Revisit the Action Steps at the end of each chapter and make sure you've at least tried each one.

- Use the Bonus Checklists as a regular tool.

- Keep this book handy as a reference. Tax credit rules might change, but the strategic mindset will always be useful. Update the specifics as needed (even write in the margins or note pages when you learn something new that builds on the information provided).

- Celebrate your wins. When you increase your profit margin, or successfully claim a tax credit for the first time, take a moment to acknowledge that. Maybe even literally give yourself a "bonus" from the savings or treat your team to lunch. It reinforces the behavior and feels good!

About the Author

Melanie E. Lewis is a nationally respected business strategist, tax expert, and founder of iPhoenix Financial Tax Group and the Empowered Dominion Network (EDN). With over 25 years of experience in finance, marketing, and business development, Melanie has helped thousands of entrepreneurs' structure, grow, and sustain profitable businesses that also qualify for powerful tax incentives. A courageous breast cancer survivor and mother of three, she brings unmatched passion, insight, and authenticity to her work. Through her books, workshops, and consulting, Melanie is on a mission to equip everyday visionaries with the tools, resources, and mindset they need to build generational wealth and kingdom impact.

Photo by Breanna L. Barnes

Looking for an engaging speaker for your next business event or workshop?
Melanie E. Lewis is an expert speaker on the following topics:

- ✓ Profit-First Entrepreneurship: Practical techniques to ensure your business is profitable by design.
- ✓ Unlocking Hidden Tax Credits: A deep dive into tax incentives that business owners often overlook and how to claim them.
- ✓ Financial Empowerment for Entrepreneurs: Demystifying business finances to take control of your company's future.
- ✓ Strategic Growth Planning: How to scale your business sustainably while keeping an eye on cash flow and profit.
- ✓ Tax Law Changes Made Simple: Breaking down recent tax changes and what they mean for small businesses (ideal for year-end seminars)
- ✓ Faith & Finance: Walking in Purpose and Profit
- ✓ Maximize Your Business Profits & Unlock Tax Credits
- ✓ Kingdom Business: Building with Integrity
- ✓ Women in Business: From Setback to Success

To inquire about speaking engagements or consulting
Booking & Contact Information:

Email: support@edn.services
Phone: 844-JOIN-EDN (844-564-6336)
Booking: Calendly.com/edn-support

www.ingramcontent.com/pod-product-compliance
Lightning Source LLC
Chambersburg PA
CBHW081258170426
43198CB00017B/2841